Booker T. Washington
Father of Tuskegee

Booker spent the first nine years of his life as a slave on the James Burroughs plantation near Roanoke, Virginia.

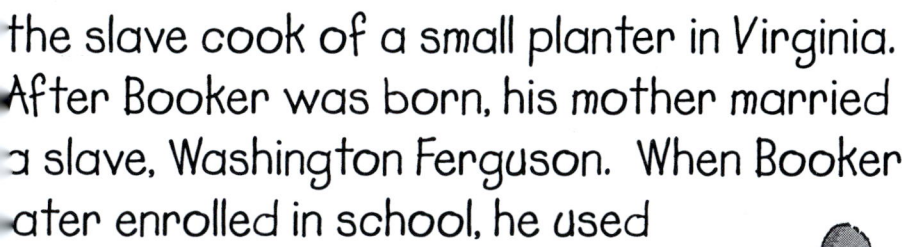

Booker T. Washington was born "Booker Taliaferro" on April 5, 1856. He was the child of an unknown white man and the slave cook of a small planter in Virginia. After Booker was born, his mother married a slave, Washington Ferguson. When Booker later enrolled in school, he used "Washington" as his last name.

The "T" in Booker T. Washington's name stands for what?

Taliaferro

Timothy

Thomas

When slavery ended in 1865, Booker's mother took her children and moved to Malden, West Virginia. Bookers' stepfather had found work in the salt mines there. Booker worked in the salt and coal mines of West Virginia for three years.

How old was Booker when he started working in the salt mines? Solve the math problem to find out!

    1865 (year started mining)
  - 1856 (year born)
    _____
        (age at beginning work)

While working in the salt mines, Booker saw strange markings on the salt barrels. He learned that these markings were numbers and letters and he became determined to read.

Pop Quiz!

1. Booker was born in:
   - ○ Maryland
   - ○ Georgia
   - ○ Virginia

2. Booker worked in what type of mine?
   - ○ salt
   - ○ granite
   - ○ gold

3. Booker was the principal of what Alabama school?
   - ○ Auburn
   - ○ Tuskegee Institute
   - ○ Alabama University

4. Booker advised many:
   - ○ presidents
   - ○ mothers
   - ○ musicians

5. Booker's autobiography is called:
   - ○ My Life as a Slave
   - ○ Up From Slavery
   - ○ Times at Tuskegee

Glossary

advice: opinion given as to what or how to do something

criticized: judged; found fault with

equality: having the same political, social, and economic rights and duties

inspiration: something or someone that inspires thought or action

mines: large holes in the earth from which minerals and rocks are dug

reputation: what people generally think about the character of a person or thing

Booker T. Washington died on November 14, 1915, at the age of 59. He became ill while in New York City, but was able to return home to Tuskegee to die. His funeral was attended by some 8,000 people! He has been, and still remains, an inspiration for generations of black Americans.

Color the picture.

Booker T. Washington is buried near George Washington Carver at Tuskegee Institute.

Not everyone agreed with Booker's belief that black people should be more concerned with learning skills than fighting for civil rights. In fact, many important leaders in the black community often criticized him. However, they could not challenge his accomplishments.

Booker was highly respected by many presidents. They asked him for advice on race relations.

Beginning with E, cross off every other letter. The letters left over will spell the name of one of the presidents who relied on Booker T. Washington for advice.

E T H E J D B D I Y W R P O
C O X S K E F V J E I L M T

___ ___ ___ ___ ___ ___ ___ ___ ___ ___ ___

Under Booker's leadership, Tuskegee grew from nothing to a world-famous center for agricultural research.

Booker gained popularity in 1895, when he was invited to speak at the International Exposition in Atlanta. After this speech, his political power, with both blacks and whites grew. He was in much demand as a speaker around the country. Tuskegee Institute continued to grow from Booker's efforts and the reputation of the school.

Color the speaker.

Booker T. Washington wrote several books. His most popular book was about his own life, called *Up From Slavery*. What is the word for this type of a book? Circle the answer.

autobiography
mystery
comic book

Booker hired George Washington Carver to teach at Tuskegee. Both men contributed to Tuskegee's good reputation.

Page 8 ©Carole Marsh/Gallopade International/800-536-2GET/www.1000readers.com
This page is not reproducible.

Most of the new buildings at Tuskegee were built by student labor. The students made their own furniture, cared for the crops and livestock, cooked, cleaned, and did their own laundry. Booker believed that by learning practical skills, blacks could quickly gain economic equality with whites.

MANNERS   MONEY   SOUTH

B	J	S	D	I
W	A	R	B	A
N	T	E	C	X
C	Q	N	T	W
U	O	N	K	Z
E	Z	A	H	J
J	R	M	B	L
P	H	L	N	K
S	Y	U	P	M
K	V	B	Q	U

Over time, Booker became well-known as a speaker on education and the future of black people.

Little by little, Booker built Tuskegee. He was a believer in life skills, such as carpentry, farming, and homemaking. He also taught personal hygiene (cleanliness) and manners, and tried to "build good character" in his students.

Find the words in the Word Find below.

Booker traveled across the country to raise money for Tuskegee. He met many rich northern millionaires who were concerned about the future of black people in the South.

Color the luggage.

EQUALITY		SKILLS		STUDENT
M	O	N	E	Y
L	X	P	O	T
S	T	U	D	E
S	E	V	N	K
Q	K	R	U	I
A	C	I	S	A
N	Y	D	L	T
O	S	I	R	L
H	T	U	O	S
Y	N	J	W	C

In 1881, some people in Alabama asked General Armstrong to recommend a principal for a new school that they were starting for blacks. He suggested Booker T. Washington. When Booker arrived in Tuskegee, Alabama, he was only 25 years old!

The people in Alabama were expecting General Armstrong to recommend a white teacher, but he didn't! He knew Booker was the man for the job!

To learn the name of the new school in Alabama, solve the code below!

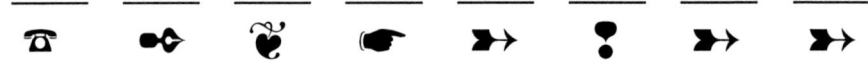

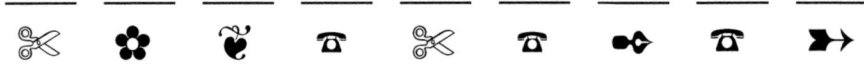

Booker found that the only school building at Tuskegee was a shack that was lent to him by a black church!

While at the Hampton Normal and Agricultural Institute, Booker met General Samuel C. Armstrong. General Armstrong was a Northerner who encouraged Booker to work hard and learn. After Booker graduated, he moved back to West Virginia to teach. Not long after, General Armstrong hired Booker to return to Hampton as a teacher.

Put the following list of events in order.

____ Booker and his family moved to West Virginia.

____ Booker was born into slavery in Virginia.

____ Booker went to work in a salt mine.

____ Booker entered an all-black school in Hampton.

In addition to teaching, Booker was in charge of 75 Native American students. He also ran a night school for poor students.

After working a full day, many black mine workers would attend school at night. Children and adults would sit side by side as they learned! A few years later, Booker heard about a school for blacks in Hampton, Virginia. At age 16, he set off for Hampton by himself.

Unscramble the sentences below to learn more about Booker T. Washington!

When _____ reached Hampton, he
         OEOBKR

had no _____. He worked as
         ONMEY

a _____ to earn his keep.
         ORJANTI

The trip to Hampton was 500 miles! Booker went partly by train, and the rest on foot.

Color the boots.